THE LITTLE BOOK OF

AGA TIPS²

RICHARD MAGGS

THE LITTLE BOOK OF AGA TIPS 2

RICHARD MAGGS

A.
Absolute Press

Absolute Press
Scarborough House, 29 James Street West
Bath BA1 2BT, England
Phone 44 (0) 1225 316013 **Fax** 44 (0) 1225 445836
E-mail info@absolutepress.co.uk
Web www.absolutepress.co.uk

First published in Great Britain in 2003
Reprinted 2004

A catalogue record of this book is available from the British Library

ISBN 1 904573 04 5

Printed and bound in Italy by Lego Print

'The secret of the fullest success
of the Aga cooker lies in the knowledge
of making the utmost use of the various
parts of which it is composed.'

Ambrose Heath

Good Food on the Aga, 1933

1

When cooking on an Aga remember that **temperature control** is completely automatic – simply place foods in the appropriate position in the cooker. There is a strong gradient of temperature between the top of the roasting oven and the bottom of the simmering oven.

2

Use buttermilk to make a stack of deliciously light **American-style pancakes** on the simmering plate. These are fantastic with real maple syrup (warmed in a jug on the top plate). Serve with crisply grilled bacon cooked at the top of the roasting oven.

3

Remember the Aga 80:20 rule.

80% of your cooking should take place in the ovens, 20% – typically things which take less than seven minutes – on the hotplates. There are a few exceptions which take longer, where constant supervision is essential, such as when boiling jam for a set.

4

Always place your

Aga kettle on the hotplate

with a slight twisting action to ensure perfect contact. To boil efficiently keep free from scale. To ensure continued peak performance, get into the habit of regularly descaling your kettle with an approved product.

5

Keep your hotplates free of toast crumbs and the like, by brushing with the wire brush supplied with your Aga.

Absolutely clean hotplates

are essential to ensure efficient heat transfer to kettles and saucepans.

6

When drying **sheets,**
duvet covers and jeans over the rail of your Aga, turn after a couple of hours and they

will scarcely need ironing.

Make sure that the air vents for the burner are not covered up on oil, gas and solid fuel models.

7

Discover the joy of

Agalinks,

Aga's very own Internet lifestyle portal. Point your browser to www.agalinks.com for the very latest Aga owners' news and content, including the cooking and kitchen section.

8

When cooking **foods that** tend to **splatter,**

push the roasting tin or cast iron dish towards the very back of the roasting oven. This makes full use of the oven capacity and helps keep the door lining clean.

9

The boiling plate recuperates fastest after use.

Par-boil potatoes and root vegetables here before draining to finish cooking covered in the simmering oven. Fast boiling of other vegetables is best on the boiling plate. Partially offset the pan if necessary to adjust the cooking rate.

10

When cooking lots of

food requiring a **high temperature**

in the roasting oven, such as for a roast meal, avoid over-using the simmering plate except for essential tasks such as heating milk and making sauces. Keeping the simmering plate lid down minimises heat loss from the oven.

11

Aga-baked beetroot

is a revelation. Take fresh, scrubbed beets and seal loosely in a double thickness of foil after adding salt, pepper and a mere drizzle of oil. Bake on the grid shelf on the floor of the roasting oven for between 45 minutes and 1¼ hours. Test regularly with a skewer until tender and peel while still warm.

12

When **drying or airing washing** on the simmering plate lid, make sure you don't cover the coil spring handle otherwise it will become too hot when you try to lift it after removing the washing.

13

Pepper skins

can be **blistered** at the very top of the roasting oven, or skin-side down in the Aga toaster on the boiling plate, before being left to sweat and cool in a plastic bag. Slip off the blackened skins over a plate to catch any juices.

14

For the

ultimate fresh continental breakfast,

defrost some frozen uncooked croissants in the refrigerator overnight covered with clingfilm. They will prove slowly, ready to cook in just seven minutes in the middle of the roasting oven the following morning.

15

On a two or three oven Aga, it is sometimes useful to **divide** the simmering oven with the solid plain shelf **ahead of time,** such as when cooking a roast meal. Place foods requiring further cooking above, use the lower half to keep cooked foods hot and to warm dishes.

16

Wipe up spills promptly as they happen with a damp cloth, especially with acidic liquids such as milk and fruit juice.

Clean as you go

is the key to keeping your Aga pristine.

17

For perfect

Crème Brûlée caramel,

take 1 oz (25g) of granulated sugar per portion and just enough water to dissolve it in a heavy pan on the simmering plate. When clear, transfer and boil rapidly on the boiling plate. When deeply golden, pour over the thoroughly chilled custard. Chill again before serving.

18

Freeze **Brazil nuts** for four hours, then bake for eight minutes on a tray on the grid shelf on the floor of the roasting oven. Cool then crack carefully. The whole kernels will then be easy to extract intact.

19

To cook whole salmon and turbot

season the cavity well and add some aromatics such as herbs and lemon. Butter liberally and wrap well in several layers of foil. Set in the roasting tin and pour $\frac{1}{4}$ inch of boiling water around the fish. Cook at the top of the roasting oven for 10 minutes per inch of thickness, plus 5 minutes.

20

When **stir-frying** with an Aga wok, preheat the empty wok on the simmering plate for a minute or two before transferring to the boiling plate ready for producing **a stylish, fast meal.**

21

The Aga Cake Baker is

a universal pan.

It bakes cakes which require over 45 minutes cooking in a two oven Aga,

boils hams and fowls,

simmers stock

and **makes** small batches of

preserves.

22

Use the Aga Cake Baker to

steam puddings

as the internal carrier makes removing

hot puddings **a safe**

and easy task.

Bring to the boil then allow 30 minutes covered on the simmering plate before transferring pan, water and pudding to the simmering oven to finish cooking.

23

When the cold plain shelf has been used in the roasting oven to shield food cooking below from over-browning, after 40 minutes the area above will in fact have a concentration of heat

ideal for Yorkshire puddings.

24

When using **the Aga toaster,** to prevent fouling the hinge, place the toaster on the boiling plate with the handle to the left. Cooking with the lid down produces toast crisp on the outside and fluffy within... leaving the lid up gives a crisper centre.

25

Poaching smoked fish in milk

with a knob of butter brings out its full flavour, especially with haddock. Use a roasting tin on a grid shelf on the floor of the roasting oven. All the fishy odours are vented away so your house won't smell of fish.

26

The Aga cast sauté pan

is a brilliant all-purpose utensil. The ground base heats up rapidly, it fits in the ovens, and the high sides contain splatters. The lid also converts it into a useful everyday casserole.

27

To cook flat fish such as **Dover Sole, plaice and dabs,** brush both sides with melted butter and grill at the top of the roasting oven using the grill rack in the high position in an Aga roasting tin. Cook the presentation side last.

28

Expand your armoury.

Consider investing in extra half size and full size Aga roasting tins, and possibly further plain and grid shelves for increased versatility.

29

Make delicious **Melba toast**

using medium-sliced bread direct on the simmering plate. Cool, cut off the crusts, and then place on a board. With a sharp serrated knife de-crust and cut each slice horizontally into two thin halves. Turn these over and finish off for a few minutes on a tray low down in the roasting oven.

30

When **planning your new kitchen,**

try to fit in an airing space fitted with telescopic rails to the side of your Aga for hand and tea towels. This is also a good place to store the larger Aga oven accessories that won't fit in your kitchen cupboards.

31

To easily open oysters, place on a grill rack in an Aga roasting tin, with $^1/_4$ inch of boiling water below. Place on the lowest set of runners in the roasting oven for 3-5 minutes. This will make them start to open and they will be a doddle to shuck.

32

Take the chill off

red wine from your cellar

by placing the opened bottle on a folded cloth for a short while at the back of the Aga. Be careful not to over-warm, however – the term *to chambré* was coined long before central heating warmed our houses....

33

When making **large casseroles and stews,** coat the meat in seasoned flour in the usual way. Then brown in batches in a little oil in the large roasting tin on the floor of the roasting oven. Keep a careful watch, tossing every few minutes. Be careful not to overcrowd the tin or they will steam rather than brown.

34

Seeds can be toasted in a heavy pan on the floor of the roasting oven. They cook very quickly so keep a watchful eye on them.

Try serving **toasted pumpkin or sunflower seeds** with pre-dinner drinks, lightly salted, as a change from peanuts.

35

Dry out mushrooms and **apple rings** overnight in the simmering and warming ovens, but remember to leave the door ajar. Prior to drying them, soak the peeled and sliced apple rings in acidulated water for 5 minutes to prevent them going brown. Make up the water using 2 teaspoons of Vitamin C powder per pint of warm water.

36

The full size roasting tin together with a full size baking tray as a lid can be used as a cooking vessel for many large-scale cooking projects in the Aga ovens –

perfect for party catering.

37

Everyday stock is really easy.

Place a chicken carcass in a pan along with a clean unpeeled and halved onion, some sliced carrot, together with a stick of celery if available and a few peppercorns. Cover with water and bring to a simmer on the top and then place covered in the simmering oven for several hours. Strain, cool and freeze.

38

If you keep poultry, dry your **used egg shells** in a tin in the simmering oven and crush very finely before incorporating back into your fowls' diet to save buying fresh oyster shell.

39

When making

fresh pasta at home,

hang finished strands over a clean Aga handrail to dry before cooking or use a purpose-made pasta drying rack set on a cloth on top of the simmering plate lid.

40

Irish soda bread

is a great Aga store cupboard standby

for emergencies

– fantastic with home-made soup. Keep the sieved dry ingredients ready-weighed out in an airtight container or buy a mix ready-made.

41

Delicious lemon curd,

without stirring, is made by placing the grated rind and juice of a warmed lemon in a Pyrex jug, with 2 oz (50g) butter and 6 oz (150g) caster sugar. Heat, covered, in the simmering oven for 30 minutes. Add 1 egg and 3 yolks and whisk for 1 minute with an electric or rotary whisk before returning, covered, for 1-2 hours.

42

Make your own **golden breadcrumbs** by drying out stale white bread overnight in the simmering oven. Blitz afterwards in a food processor.

43

Runny honey that has become crystallised may be rendered **clear again** by placing the opened jar at the back of the top plate of the Aga for a few hours.

44

When entertaining,

pre-heat your empty vegetable tureens in the simmering oven for an hour, using plates as lids. Par-boil root vegetables and potatoes and drain to then finish cooking in the hot tureens in the simmering oven. Allow a little longer than usual.

45

Learn how to make use of

every cubic inch of your simmering oven.

Determine which combination of your pans can be stacked most efficiently and packed to best effect. Use enamelled or Pyrex plates as spacers where necessary and keep handles pointing in the same direction for ease of use.

46

When the simmering oven is completely full of food cooking, **allow a longer** composite **cooking time** than for when cooking with just a couple of pans, especially in the case of potatoes and root vegetables.

47

Purchase a cheap

meat-roasting thermometer

in order to determine accurately when meat is cooked to the stage you like. This takes the guesswork out of testing and ensures that a thorough cook is achieved preventing any risk of food poisoning.

48

The **baking quality** of the Aga oven castings is the nearest thing to **a traditional baker's brick oven.** With a trusty KitchenAid mixer the results far surpass loaves from a bread machine. Bread making is easily incorporated into your weekly routine, it really is a matter of minutes once mastered.

49

Not sure where to cook

fast food for children?

Grill chicken nuggets and fish fingers in a tin on the first set of runners. Cook oven chips in a tray on the floor of the roasting oven. Baked beans heat through beautifully in an hour in a covered shallow dish on the floor of the simmering oven.

50

Heat a **terracotta tile** in the roasting oven for five or six minutes. Then place in the base of your

breadbasket

under freshly baked or warmed rolls. Send to the table at the last minute and they will keep **warm** until required.

Acknowledgments

My thanks to all my family, friends, colleagues, fellow chefs and of course every Aga owner for their constant support and encouragement. To everyone at Aga-Rayburn; it is a pleasure to work with such an enthusiastic group of people. Also a huge thank you to my publisher, Jon Croft and editor and graphic designer, Matt Inwood at Absolute Press who are now great friends and Aga devotees.

AGA is a registered trademark of
Aga Foodservice Group plc.

Bake-O-Glide™ is a re-usable non-stick coated cooking material, available from Aga Specialists.

Richard Maggs

A dynamic and accomplished chef, Richard is an authority on Aga cookery. As well as having featured on TV and radio, he has written for several food magazines, and contributes a regular column to the official Aga Magazine. He is also the resident Aga cookery expert, The Cookery Doctor, with the award-winning Agalinks website at www.agalinks.com.

His first *Little Book of Aga Tips* turned him, overnight, into a bestselling author.

A selected list of Aga titles from Absolute Press

Richard Maggs' *Aga Tips* titles
The bestselling Aga Tips *series: indispensable for every Aga owner.*

The Little Book of Aga Tips (2.99)
The Little Book of Aga Tips 2 (2.99)
The Little Book of Rayburn Tips (2.99)

Tim James
Aga: The Story of a Kitchen Classic (£30)
The beautifully illustrated, definitive 80-year history of a kitchen icon.

Louise Walker's *Traditional Aga* titles
The bestselling Traditional Aga *series: essential for every Aga cook.*

The Traditional Aga Cookery Book (£9.95)
The Traditional Aga Party Book (£9.95)
The Traditional Aga Book of Slow Cooking (£9.95)
The Traditional Aga Box Set (*all three titles above*) (£29.50)
The Traditional Aga Four Seasons Cookery Book (£9.95)
The Traditional Aga Book of Vegetarian Cooking (£9.95)

Laura James' New Aga Cook books
A contemporary collection of recipes for today's Aga cook.

The New Aga Cook: Fast (7.99)
The New Aga Cook: Kids (7.99)
The New Aga Cook: Weekends (7.99)

THE LITTLE BOOK OF AGA TIPS

'Full of winning ideas for Aga owners.'
The Times

'Aga Tips is splendid! The best tip is about warming immovable jam jar lids – brilliant!'
Marjorie Dunkels, Aga owner